Lerner SPORTS

SPORTS ALL-ST★RS

SLOANE STEPHENS

Jon M. Fishman

Lerner Publications • Minneapolis

Copyright © 2020 by Lerner Publishing Group, Inc.

All rights reserved. International copyright secured. No part of this book may be reproduced, stored in a retrieval system, or transmitted in any form or by any means—electronic, mechanical, photocopying, recording, or otherwise—without the prior written permission of Lerner Publishing Group, Inc., except for the inclusion of brief quotations in an acknowledged review.

Lerner Publications Company
An imprint of Lerner Publishing Group, Inc.
241 First Avenue North
Minneapolis, MN 55401 USA

For reading levels and more information, look up this title at www.lernerbooks.com.

Main body text set in Albany Std. Typeface provided by Agfa.

Library of Congress Cataloging-in-Publication Data

Names: Fishman, Jon M., author.
Title: Sloane Stephens / Jon M. Fishman.
Description: Minneapolis : Lerner Publications, [2020] | Series: Sports all-stars | Includes bibliographical references and index. | Audience: Ages: 7–11 | Audience: Grades: 4–6 | Summary: "All-court tennis phenom Sloane Stephens is ranked fourth in the WTA with six singles titles and one US Open Championship. Find out more about this WTA superstar!"— Provided by publisher.
Identifiers: LCCN 2019026112 (print) | LCCN 2019026113 (ebook) | ISBN 9781541577282 (hardcover) | ISBN 9781541589582 (paperback) | ISBN 9781541583603 (ebook)
Subjects: LCSH: Stephens, Sloane, 1993-—Juvenile literature. | African American women tennis players—Biography—Juvenile literature. | Tennis—United States—Juvenile literature.
Classification: LCC GV994.S625 F57 2020 (print) | LCC GV994.S625 (ebook) | DDC 796.342089/96073—dc23

LC record available at https://lccn.loc.gov/2019026112
LC ebook record available at https://lccn.loc.gov/2019026113

Manufactured in the United States of America
1-46750-47741-9/17/2019

CONTENTS

GETTING THROUGH

Sloane Stephens prepares to hit a powerful serve.

Rain poured onto the tennis courts in Charleston, South Carolina. The wet, cold weather delayed play for about three hours.

FACTS
AT A GLANCE

- **Date of Birth:** March 20, 1993

- **Position:** tennis player

- **League: Women's Tennis Association (WTA)**

- **Professional Highlights:** became a pro tennis player at the age of 16; won her first WTA **tournament** in 2015; won the 2017 US Open

- **Personal Highlights:** began playing tennis at the age of nine; helps kids live healthful lives; earned a college degree in 2017

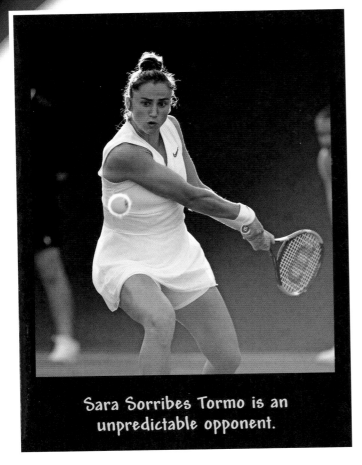
Sara Sorribes Tormo is an unpredictable opponent.

When Sloane Stephens finally began her **match**, she didn't seem ready. She hit shots out of bounds and into the net. She fell behind Sara Sorribes Tormo in the first **set**, five **games** to two.

Stephens and Sorribes Tormo were playing in the Volvo Car Open tournament on April 2, 2019. Stephens won the 2016 open in Charleston. But after the long rain delay in 2019, she was off to a slow start.

Stephens came roaring back. She used all of her skills and experience to come from behind. Sorribes Tormo **served**, and Stephens crushed the return. The two players drilled the ball back and forth with power.

Suddenly, Stephens hit a soft shot. Her opponent had to rush to the net to stop the ball from bouncing twice. She hit it back to Stephens, who smacked a long shot. Sorribes Tormo raced away from the net to get the ball. When it came to Stephens again, she hit an even softer shot. Sorribes Tormo sprinted, but this time, she couldn't get there in time. Stephens won four games in a row to take a 6–5 lead in the set.

Sorribes Tormo had lost the lead, but she hadn't given up. She came back to tie the first set, 6–6. That meant it went to a **tiebreak**. Stephens reached seven points first to win the tiebreak.

The second set also went to a tiebreak. Stephens trailed by two points before winning five points in a row. That gave her victory in the tiebreak, the set, and the match.

The match had lasted more than two and a half hours. It had been a long struggle against a tough opponent. But Stephens was pleased that her hard work had kept her in the tournament. "It was a tough day, and I was just happy to get through," she said.

Sloane serves in the 2009 French Open.

Sloane Stephens was born in Plantation, Florida, on March 20, 1993. People who knew her family could have guessed that Sloane would become a superstar athlete.

The National Football League named John Stephens the 1988 Offensive Rookie of the Year.

Her mother, Sybil Smith, competed on Boston University's swimming team in the 1980s. She became the first black woman to win All-American honors as one of the nation's top swimmers. Sloane's father, John Stephens, played pro football for the New England Patriots from 1988 to 1992.

Smith saw Sloane's potential early on.

Sloane began walking when she was nine months old. The way she moved convinced her mother that Sloane could be a great athlete someday. "She had a natural balance about her," Smith said.

Sloane's parents divorced soon after she was born. When she was two, Sloane moved with her mother to Fresno, California. Smith married Sheldon Farrell in 1997.

The couple played tennis, and they introduced Sloane to the sport when she was nine. Her natural skills made her stand out on the court. A year later, the family moved to Florida so Sloane could train at tennis **academies** there.

In Florida, Sloane dedicated her life to tennis, and it showed. She still had her natural balance. She also had dazzling speed and powerful shots. She improved so quickly that she was ready to join the Women's Tennis Association full-time in 2009 at the age of 16.

The WTA season has almost 60 tennis events in dozens of countries around the world. The season includes the four main Grand Slam tournaments: the Australian Open, the French Open, Wimbledon (in England), and the US Open.

Stephens celebrates winning the 2015 Citi Open.

WTA players compete for millions of dollars in prize money. Playing professionally, Stephens was up against the best players in the world. She won some matches, but she always lost before a tournament's final rounds. Five years passed, and she still hadn't won a WTA tournament.

In August 2015, Stephens played at the Citi Open in Washington, DC. It was her 84th WTA tournament. For the first time, she made it to the final round. She crushed her opponent 6–1, 6–2 in a match that lasted just 63 minutes. Stephens was the champion! "Nothing was stopping me today," she said.

A SWEAT

Stephens has laser-like focus.

Stephens's first WTA win was the result of years of tennis practice. It also had a lot to do with her natural strength and **agility**.

Stephens hired Sven Groeneveld as her coach in 2019.

Her mother noticed Stephens's balance when she took her first steps. A few years later, her classmates noticed her strength. "In the fourth grade, I remember people would ask why I had so many muscles," she said.

Tennis players must be physically fit to play matches that last for two hours or more. As Stephens grew and pursued her tennis career, she began to strengthen her muscles. She works out for two hours a day, five days a week.

For the first hour, Stephens does exercises to improve her agility. She quickly steps through a grid that looks like a ladder on the ground. She hops through the grid on one leg. Then she jumps in and out of the grid as she moves forward.

Stephens also improves her strength and agility by completing a series of jumps. She jumps onto boxes or benches or jumps over plastic cones. Jumping gives muscles a special workout by strengthening and stretching them at the same time.

Fast-paced exercises get Stephens ready to dominate the court.

For the second hour, Stephens lifts heavy weights. The focus on strength training helps her smash blazing shots during matches. After, she heads to the court for two hours of tennis practice. "From the time I get up, I'm working out and sweating," she said.

Challenging practices keep Stephens at the top of her game.

Sometimes, Stephens plays several WTA matches in a row without breaks. At those times, she gets most of her exercise on the court. Working out for hours might make her too tired to play matches. She does lighter workouts with elastic bands and other gear.

Stephens eats healthful food to fuel her active life. She likes to snack throughout the day to avoid feeling tired and hungry. She eats different nuts and fruits, and she loves cheese. She usually carries snacks with her so she can grab a bite whenever she needs to.

STEPPING UP OFF THE COURT

Stephens fires the ball back to her opponent.

Stephens and her foundation help kids get dental exams.

As a tennis superstar, Stephens makes a lot of money. She has won more than $13 million in prize money at WTA events. She earns millions more by representing companies such as Nike and Colgate.

Stephens playing in a tournament in Spain

Stephens knows she won't be able to play pro tennis forever. That's why she keeps close track of her money. She doesn't want to run out after her career is finished. But she still indulges once in a while. She likes to get her nails styled or treat herself to things she likes at stores such as Target.

Pro players must be away from home for much of the tennis season. They travel to tournaments all around the world. Between competing and traveling, life on the road can wear down players. When Stephens has time off, she likes to relax at home. Out of the spotlight, she can unwind and get ready for the next trip.

Growing Her Game

In 2016, Stephens injured her left foot. She had surgery in January 2017 and spent months unable to play tennis. But she didn't sit around feeling sorry for herself. She took college writing and media classes online. In 2017, she graduated!

While she couldn't play, Stephens also joined the Tennis Channel and appeared on TV. She talked about WTA matches and players and gave viewers an inside look at tennis. The job helped Stephens see tennis in different ways and gave her new ideas about how to play.

Stephens (*second from left*) talks tennis with other athletes.

Stephens's foundation helps kids learn how to play tennis.

Stephens spends time giving back to the community. The Sloane Stephens Foundation helps young people lead healthful lifestyles. The foundation works to give children a bright future through programs that help with schoolwork or offer tennis lessons.

The foundation rebuilt tennis courts in Compton, California, in 2018. Stephens gave tennis lessons to hundreds of kids in the area, and the foundation holds tennis camps there each summer. It also helps kids prepare for the Special Olympics. The Special Olympics encourages kids of all abilities to play sports.

In 2019, Stephens was named a finalist for the Muhammad Ali Sports Humanitarian of the Year Award. Each year, the award goes to an athlete who has made a positive impact on the community through sports. Hard work has made Stephens rich and famous. She wants to give more kids the chance to reach their own tennis dreams.

The Special Olympics celebrates athletes with disabilities.

SLAM

Stephens during the 2015 Citi Open

When Stephens won the Citi Open in 2015, she proved that she could win a WTA tournament. But it wasn't a Grand Slam. Most fans judge the greatest tennis players by how they do in Grand Slam events. They're the most popular tournaments of the year, and players compete for the biggest prizes.

Stephens blasts the ball during the 2019 French Open.

Sloane Stephens is ranked a top player in the US. But in 2017, her world ranking sank after her foot surgery. She returned to the court in July for Wimbledon and lost in the first round. When she began warm-up matches for the US Open in August, she was ranked 957th in the world.

Venus Williams has won seven Grand Slams.

Stephens had worked hard to recover from surgery. The work started paying off. She beat player after player at the 2017 US Open, including ninth-ranked Venus Williams. Stephens made it to the final match and beat US player Madison Keys 6–3, 6–0. Stephens was the US Open champion! "BEST. DAY. EVER." she wrote on Twitter.

While Sloane Stephens was the top-ranked US player in the WTA during the 2019 Wimbledon tournament, she has never ranked first in the world. Her highest world ranking was third in July 2018.

Stephens has won six WTA events in her career. She's won more than twice as many Grand Slam matches as she's lost. Yet she hasn't been able to win a Grand Slam tournament since the US Open. With her natural talent and hard work on and off the court, it's just a matter of time before she becomes a Grand Slam champion again.

Stephens looks forward to building off of her success.

All-Star Stats

It took Stephens a long time to win her first **WTA** event. But combining her natural talent with a lot of effort has made her one of the world's top players. Take a look at where Stephens ranked on the **WTA** world rankings in 2019 during the Wimbledon tournament.

WTA Ranking Players and Home Country

1. Ashleigh Barty, Australia
2. Naomi Osaka, Japan
3. Karolina Pliskova, Czech Republic
4. Kiki Bertens, The Netherlands
5. Angelique Kerber, Germany
6. Petra Kvitova, Czech Republic
7. Simona Halep, Romania
8. Elina Svitolina, Ukraine
9. **Sloane Stephens, United States**
10. Serena Williams, United States
11. Aryna Sabalenka, Belarus
12. Anastasija Sevastova, Latvia
13. Belinda Bencic, Switzerland
14. Marketa Vondrousova, Czech Republic
15. Qiang Wang, China

Source Notes

7 "Stephens Staves Off Sorribes Tormo in Charleston Second Round," WTA Tennis, April 2, 2019, https://www.wtatennis.com/news/stephens-staves-sorribes-tormo-charleston-second-round.

10 Nila Do Simon, "Sloane Stephens: Love Game," *Flamingo*, February 25, 2019, https://www.flamingomag.com/2019/02/25/sloane-stephens/.

12 Peter Bodo, "Sloane Stephens' Citi Open Win a Long Time Coming," *ESPN*, August 10, 2015, http://www.espn.com/tennis/story/_/id/13407482/sloane-stephens-citi-open-win-long-coming.

14 Simon, "Sloane Stephens: Love Game."

16 Pam O'Brien, "The Thing That Helps Sloane Stephens Become a Ninja on the Tennis Court," *Shape*, March 13, 2018, https://www.shape.com/celebrities/interviews/sloane-stephens-become-ninja-tennis-court.

26 Jill Martin, "Unseeded American Sloane Stephens Wins US Open for First Major Title," *CNN*, September 10, 2017, https://www.cnn.com/2017/09/09/tennis/us-open-final-madison-keys-sloane-stephens/index.html.

Glossary

academies: schools that teach special skills

agility: ability to move easily and quickly

games: parts of a set that are won when a player wins at least four points

Grand Slam: the name given to the four most important pro tennis tournaments: the Australian Open, the French Open, Wimbledon (in England), and the US Open

match: a tennis contest.

served: hit the ball to begin play

set: a group of six or more games

tiebreak: a special game to decide a winner if a set is tied 6–6

tournament: a series of matches to decide a champion

Women's Tennis Association (WTA): the governing body of women's pro tennis

Further Information

Braun, Eric. *Incredible Sports Trivia: Fun Facts and Quizzes*. Minneapolis: Lerner Publications, 2018.

Ellenport, Craig. *Sloane Stephens*. New York: Aladdin, 2019.

Fishman, Jon M. *Serena Williams*. Minneapolis: Lerner Publications, 2017.

Sloane Stephens Foundation
https://sloanestephensfoundation.org/

Sloane Stephens—WTA Tennis
https://www.wtatennis.com/players/player/315683/title/sloane
-stephens%20

US Open
https://www.usopen.org/index.html

Index

Photo Acknowledgments

Image credits: Alex Grimm/Getty Images, p. 4; Mike Hewitt/Getty Images, p. 6; Matthew Stockman/Getty Images, p. 8; Mitchell Layton/Getty Images, p. 9; Volkan Furuncu/Anadolu Agency/Getty Images, p. 10; Patrick Smith/Getty Images, pp. 12, 18, 24; Clive Brunskill/Getty Images, pp. 13, 26; Julian Finney/Getty Images, pp. 14, 16; iStock/Getty Images, p. 15; jenifoto/Getty Images, p. 17; Rich Fury/Getty Images, p. 19; Alex Pantling/Getty Images, p. 20; Craig Barritt/Getty Images, p. 21; SolStock/ Getty Images, p. 22; ROBYN BECK/AFP/Getty Images, p. 23; Quality Sport Images/ Getty Images, p. 25; TPN/Getty Images, p. 27.

Cover image: Mark Metcalfe/Getty Images.